Recipes for Making Wine from Fruit and Vegetables at Home

by

C. Shepherd

British Library Cataloguing-in-Publication Data
A catalogue record for this book is available from
the British Library

Contents

HOME MADE WINES

THE QUANTITIES given in these recipes must be regarded only as a standard. They may be halved, doubled, and so on, according to the amount of wine one intends to make.

Further, the stated period during which wine is to stand before bottling, and the length of time to elapse before using it, may both be varied somewhat by the individual. As already mentioned, there are few rigid rules in wine-making.

APPLE WINE

Ingredients.—1 gallon of mashed apples, 1 gallon of boiling water. To every pound weight of liquid, allow ½ lb. of loaf sugar.

Method.—Put the mashed apples into a basin and pour over them the boiling water. Cover with a cloth and let stand for two weeks. Strain and weigh the liquid and add sugar in the proportion stated above. Stir until the sugar has dissolved then cover the basin again. Skim off the scum which forms and leave until next day when the liquid will be ready to bottle. Cork and seal carefully.

APRICOT WINE

Ingredients.—12 lb. of sound but not over-ripe apricots. 1 lb. of loaf sugar, 1 pint of white wine, 3 gallons of water, small quantity of yeast spread on toast.

Method.—Remove the stones of the fruit, take out the kernels, and cut each apricot into 6 or 8 pieces. Put them into a preserving-pan with the water, sugar, and about half the kernels, and simmer very gently for 1 hour. Turn the whole into an earthenware vessel, let it remain undisturbed until cool, then put in the yeast on toast. (See Page 15.) Cover the vessel with a cloth, let it remain undisturbed for 3 days, then strain the liquid into a clean, dry cask, add the white wine, and bung lightly.

At the end of 6 months draw off the wine into bottles, cork them closely, store in a cool, dry place for about 12 months, and the wine will be then ready for use.

Note.—Dried apricots may be used but they must be soaked until well swollen before use.

BEETROOT WINE

Ingredients.—15 lb. beetroots, 6 pints of sloes, 4½ gallons of water, 6 lb. of sultanas, 2 oranges, 2 small lemons, 13 lb. loaf sugar, 4 tablespoonfuls of yeast, 1 pint of brandy, 3 oz. of sugar candy, 1 oz. of isinglass, and 1 oz. of bitter almonds.

Method.—Wash the beetroots well but avoid breaking the skins. Boil them slowly until tender and peel when they are cold. Crush the sloes and break the stones. Put them into a preserving pan with a quart of water and boil gently for about 20 minutes. Peel and slice the beetroots and put them into a large bowl. Pour in the strained sloe juice and cover over with a cloth. Let it stand undisturbed until next day. Then add the sultanas cut in halves, the thinly peeled rind of the lemons and oranges. Now boil the sugar in 4½ gallons of water for about 40 minutes and after skimming well pour this over the beetroots and sloes. When it is nearly cold put in the yeast on toast and cover again. Let it stand undisturbed for 3 days. Next strain the liquid carefully into a clean cask, keeping back about a gallon of the liquid to fill up the cask as fermentation subsides. As soon as the hissing ceases pour in the brandy and add the sugar candy. Now bung the cask and leave it undisturbed for a month. Rack it off and filter the lees, then return all the liquid to the cask and add the dissolved isinglass and the blanched and shredded bitter almonds.

Secure the bung and leave the wine to mature for at least 18 months. After which it may be bottled and it will then be ready for use in another 12 months.

BEETROOT WINE (A simpler method):

As the above recipe, which has been handed down from the past, is somewhat complicated, we give the following alternative:

Allow 4 lb. of beetroot to every gallon of water you propose to use. Leave them overnight in enough cold water to cover them. Then peel, and cut them into slices about an inch thick. Put them into the water and simmer for anything up to an hour, having first added a cupful of hops, several oranges and a lemon cut into quarters, and a few cloves with a piece or two of bruised ginger. (Omit the hops if difficult to obtain.) Strain, and to the liquid left add sugar in the proportion of 2 lb. of sugar to each gallon, and simmer until this is dissolved, stirring all the time. Put in yeast in the manner described earlier, see Page 15.

Ferment for about two weeks, stirring and skimming daily. Strain again and transfer to cask or stone jar and bottle in two or three months.

BLACKBERRY WINE

Ingredients.—4 gallons of sound, ripe blackberries, 4 gallons of boiling water. To every gallon of liquid allow 1 lb. of loaf sugar. To every gallon of wine allow 1 stick of cinnamon and 1 gill of brandy.

Method.—Crush the blackberries in a large bowl or tub and pour over them the boiling water. Stir well, cover with a cloth and leave undisturbed for 4 or 5 days. Without breaking up the crust which has formed on the surface strain off the liquid and measure it carefully. Add sugar in the proportion stated above and pour into a clean cask reserving about a gallon of the liquid to fill up the cask as fermentation ceases. This wine generally clears itself, but the addition of isinglass is recommended. Let it stand for about a fortnight. Then add the brandy and cinnamon, secure the bung and leave undisturbed for twelve months.

Note.—Unless the blackberries are very ripe, double the above sugar is needed.

BLACK CURRANT WINE

Ingredients.—2 gallons of fresh black currant juice, 7 lb. of loaf sugar, 2 gallons of cold water. To every 2–3 gallons of wine allow 1 pint of brandy.

Method.—Put the black currant juice, sugar and water into a clean cask. Let it stand in a warm corner until fermentation ceases. Rack the liquid off, measuring the wine in so doing and add brandy in the proportion stated above.

Secure the bung and leave undisturbed for at least 9 months. Bottle and seal and the wine will be ready for use in a year at the outside.

CHAMPAGNE, ENGLISH

Ingredients.—3 gallons of unripe yellow gooseberries, 12 lb. of loaf sugar, 3 gallons of water, 1½ pints of gin, ½ oz. of isinglass.

Method.—Top and tail the gooseberries and put them in a large pan or tub. Crush them and pour over the water. Let them remain for 48 hours, stirring from time to time meanwhile. Crush thoroughly and strain off all the liquid. Stir into this the sugar and let it stand for about three days covered by a clean cloth but stirring from time to time. Then strain the liquid into a clean cask, adding the gin and isinglass previously dissolved in a little water. Place the bung in loosely and do not secure until fermentation has ceased.

The wine should stand undisturbed in the cask for a 12 month before bottling.

CHERRY WINE

Ingredients.—12 lb. of cherries, preferably small black ones either loaf or good preserving sugar.

Method.—Place the cherries on a large dish and bruise them well with a large wooden spoon. Allow them to remain until the following day, then drain them well on a hair sieve, and measure the juice into an earthenware vessels To each quart of juice add ½ lb. of sugar, cover the vessels let it stand for 24 hours, and strain the liquor into a clean, dry cask. Bung closely, but provide the bung of the cask with a vent-peg; let it remain undisturbed for about 6 months, then drain off into bottles. Cork closely, and store in a cool, dry place.

CHERRY WINE (*Another Method*)

Ingredients.—Ripe cherries. To each quart of juice extracted from them add ½ lb. loaf sugar, a pinch each of ground mace, ground cloves and ground all-spice, ½ a pint of brandy, and ½ a pint of rum.

Method.—Stone the cherries, put them into a large jar, place in a saucepan of boiling water, and cook gently until the juice is all extracted. Then strain into a preserving pan, add sugar and flavouring ingredients in the proportion stated above, and boil and skim until clear. Let it cook, add the spirits, pour into bottles, and cork fairly closely at first.

CIDER WINE

Ingredients.—4 gallons of apple juice, 4 lb. of honey, 1 oz. white tartar, ¼ oz. each of cloves, mace and cinnamon, 1 quart of Jamaica rum.

Method.—Place the apple juice, honey and tartar, with the cloves, mace and cinnamon in a clean cask and cover the bung hole with a piece of clean cloth. Let it remain undisturbed until fermentation has ceased. Pour in the rum and fasten the bung securely. The wine will be ready for bottling in 6 months.

COLTSFOOT WINE

Ingredients.—5 gallons of freshly-gathered coltsfoot flowers, 5 lb. of stoned and chopped raisins, 6 lemons, 6 gallons of water, 12 lb. of loaf sugar, requisite yeast, 1 quart of brandy.

Method.—Boil the sugar and the strained juice of the lemons in the water for about ½ an hour, skimming from time to time as necessary. Place the coltsfoot flowers, raisins and thinly peeled rind of the lemons in a tub or large basin and pour over them the hot liquid. Stir steadily until nearly cold then stir in the yeast. Cover with a clean cloth and let it stand undisturbed for 3 or 4 days. Strain off into a clean cask, reserving 2 or 3 pints of the liquid to fill up the cask as fermentation subsides. Place the bung in lightly until the hissing has ceased, then pour in the brandy and secure the bung tightly. The wine will be ready for bottling in 6 months' time.

COWSLIP WINE

Ingredients.—4 quarts of cowslip flowers, 4 quarts of water, 3 lb. of loaf sugar, the finely-grated rind and juice of 1 orange and 1 lemon, ¼ of an oz. of dried yeast moistened with water, ¼ of a pint of brandy, if liked.

Method.—Boil the sugar and water together for ½ an hour, skimming when necessary, and pour, quite boiling, over the rinds and strained juice of the orange and lemon. Let it cool, then put in the yeast and cowslip flowers, cover with a cloth, and allow it to remain undisturbed for 48 hours. Strain and pour into a clean dry cask, add the brandy, bung closely, let it remain thus for 8 weeks, then draw it off into bottles. Cork securely, store in a cool, dry place for 3 or 4 weeks, and it will then be ready for use.

CURRANT AND RASPBERRY WINE

Ingredients.—1½ gallons of red-currant juice, 1 pint of raspberry juice, 3½ gallons of water, 6 lb. of either loaf sugar or good preserving sugar.

Method.—Extract the juice as directed in the 2 following recipes. Add to it the water and sugar, stir until the latter is dissolved, then turn the whole into a cask, and bung closely, but provide the top of the cask with a vent peg. As soon as fermentation ceases, tighten the vent peg, and let the cask remain undisturbed in a moderately warm place for 12 months. At the end of this time rack off into dry bottles, cork them closely, and seal the top with melted wax. The wine should be ready for use in about 3 months.

CURRANT CHAMPAGNE

Ingredients.—2 quarts each of red and white currants, 8 lb. of loaf sugar, 3 gallons of water, 1 gill of liquid yeast, 1 oz. of isinglass.

Method.—Boil the sugar and water together for 10 minutes, removing the scum as its rises. Place the picked and bruised currants in a tub or large bowl and pour over the hot syrup. Stir from time to time and when lukewarm pour in the yeast. Cover over with a clean cloth and allow to stand undisturbed for 3 days. Strain off the liquid into a clean cask and when the hissing has ceased pour in the dissolved isinglass. Secure the bung tightly and bottle in 8 months' time.

CURRANT WINE, RED

Ingredients.—Ripe red currants. To each gallon of fruit allow 1½ gallons of cold water, and 5 lb. either of loaf sugar or good preserving sugar, and ½ a pint of good brandy.

Method.—Remove the stalks from the currants, put them into an earthenware bowl, bruise them well with a wooden spoon, and drain off the juice. Put the juice aside, add the water to the berries, let it stand for 2 or 3 hours, stirring occasionally meanwhile. At the end of this time strain the liquid from the berries into the juice, add ¾ of the sugar, stir occasionally until dissolved, then pour the whole into a cask, filling it 3-parts full.

Bung closely, but place a vent peg in the bung of the cask, and let the cask remain for 1 month. Dissolve the remainder of the sugar in the smallest possible quantity of warm water, mix it well with the contents of the cask, replace the bung, and allow the cask to remain undisturbed for 6 weeks longer. Now drain off the wine into a clean, dry cask, add the brandy, let the cask stand for about 6 months in a dry, warm place, then bottle and cork tightly.

The wine may be used at once, but will be better if kept for 12 months at least.

DAMSON WINE

Ingredients.—To each gallon of damsons add 1 gallon of boiling water. To each gallon of liquor obtained from these add 4 lb. of loaf sugar, and ½ a pint of brandy.

Method.—Remove the stalks, put the fruit into an earthenware bowl, pour in the boiling water, and cover with a cloth. Stir the liquid 3 or 4 times daily for 4 days, then add the sugar and brandy, after straining, and when the former is dissolved turn the whole into a clean dry cask. Cover the bunghole with a cloth, folded into several thicknesses, until fermentation ceases, then bung tightly, and allow the cask to remain undisturbed for 12 months in a moderately warm place. At the end of this time it should be racked off into bottles.

The wine may be used at once, but if well corked and stored in a dry place it may be kept for years.

DAMSON WINE (*Another Method*)

Ingredients.—16 quarts of sound ripe damsons, stalked and stoned, 16 lb. of loaf sugar, 21 quarts of water, yeast, 1½ pints of brandy and 1 oz. of isinglass.

Method.—Boil the sugar and water together for 30 minutes, skimming from time to time as necessary. Put in the damsons and continue to boil for another 30 minutes, stirring and skimming as required. Strain through a fine sieve into a large bowl or tub and when quite cool put in the yeast. Cover with a clean cloth and let it remain undisturbed for 3 or 4 days. Drain off the liquid into a clean cask. Filter the lees and retain this liquid to fill up the cask with as fermentation subsides. When the hissing has entirely ceased add the brandy and secure the bung. At the end of 6

9

months the wine may be racked off and the lees filtered. Now pour the wine back into the cask and add the isinglass dissolved in a little of the wine. Secure the bung and bottle at the end of 2 years time.

Note.—Another, and slightly more encouraging recipe, advocates 10 months in the cask or jar and then 2 months in the bottle, when the wine will be matured.

DANDELION WINE

Ingredients.—4 quarts of dandelion flowers, 4 quarts of boiling water, 3 lb. of loaf sugar, 1 inch of whole ginger, 1 lemon, the thinly-pared rind of 1 orange, ¼ of an oz. of dried yeast moistened with water.

Method.—Put the petals of the flowers into a bowl, pour over them the boiling water, let the bowl remain covered for 3 days, meanwhile stirring it well and frequently. Strain the liquid into a preserving-pan, add the rinds of the orange and lemon, both of which should be pared off in thin fine strips, the sugar, ginger, and the lemon previously stripped of its white pith and thinly sliced. Boil gently for about ½ an hour, and when cool add the yeast spread on a piece of toast. Allow it to stand for 2 days, then turn it into a cask, keep it well bunged down for 8 or 9 weeks, and bottle the wine for use.

ELDERBERRY WINE

Ingredients.—7 lb. of elderberries, 3 gallons of water. To each gallon of liquid add 3 lb. of good loaf sugar, 1 lb. of raisins, ½ an oz. of ground ginger, 6 cloves, ¼ of a pint of brandy, ½ a teaspoonful of dried yeast.

Method.—Strip the berries from the stalks, pour the water, quite boiling, over them, let them stand for 24 hours, then bruise well and drain through a hair sieve or jelly-bag. Measure the juice obtained, put it into a preserving-pan with sugar, raisins, ginger, and cloves in above-stated proportions, boil gently for 1 hour, and skim when necessary. Let the liquid stand until lukewarm, then put in the yeast and turn the whole into a clean, dry, cask. Cover the bung-hole with a folded cloth, let the cask remain undisturbed for 14 days, then stir in the brandy and bung tightly.

In about 6 months the wine may be drawn off into bottles, tightly corked, and stored for use.

ELDERFLOWER WINE

Ingredients.—½ a gallon of elderflowers, 8 lb. of raisins 6 gallons of water, 16 lb. loaf sugar, dried yeast, 4 large lemons. To every gallon of wine allow ¼ pint of brandy.

Method.—Boil the water and sugar together for 10 minutes, removing the scum as its rises. Put the elderflowers into a large basin or tub with the raisins, stoned and cut up into small pieces and pour the syrup over them. Stir well and when just lukewarm put in the yeast. Cover with a clean cloth and let stand undisturbed until next day. Now add the strained juice and the thinly peeled rind of the lemons. Recover and allow to stand for 3 more days. Strain the liquid into a clean cask, reserving a small quantity to fill up with as fermentation subsides. As soon as the hissing has entirely ceased add brandy in the proportion stated above and tighten the bung. At the end of 6 months it will be ready for bottling.

GINGER WINE

Ingredients.—3 gallons of cold water, 9 lb. of loaf sugar, ¼ of a lb. of whole ginger bruised, ¼ of a lb. of raisins, the strained juice and finely-pared rinds of 4 lemons, dried yeast.

Method.—Stone and halve the raisins, put them into a large preserving-pan with the water, sugar and ginger bruised;

boil for 1 hour, skimming frequently. Add the lemon rind and turn the whole into a large earthenware bowl or wooden tub, allow the liquid to stand until luke-warm, then put in the yeast. On the following day put the preparation into a clean, dry cask, add the lemon-juice, and bung lightly. Stir the wine every day for a fortnight, then tighten the bung.

Let the wine remain undisturbed for 3 or 4 months, when it may be bottled for use.

GINGER WINE (*Another Method*)

Ingredients.—6 gallons of water, 14 lb. of loaf sugar, 6 oz. of whole ginger bruised, 6 lb. of raisins, ½ an oz. of isinglass, 6 lemons, yeast as above, 1 pint of brandy.

Method.—Remove the peel of the lemons as thinly as possible, and boil it with the water, sugar and ginger for ½ an hour. Meanwhile stone and halve the raisins, put them into an earthenware bowl, pour the liquid over them when nearly cold, add the lemon-juice and yeast. Stir it every day for a fortnight, then add the isinglass previously dissolved in a little warm water, and drain into a clean, dry cask. Let the wine remain closely bunged for about 3 months, then bottle for use.

GOOSEBERRY WINE

Ingredients.—20 lb. of firm green gooseberries, 3 gallons of hot water, 15 lb. of loaf sugar, 1½ oz. of cream of tartar.

Method.—Top and tail the gooseberries, put them into an earthenware bowl or wooden tub, and pour over them the hot water. Let them soak for 24 hours, then bruise them well with a heavy wooden mallet or spoon, and drain the juice through a fine hair sieve or jelly-bag.

Replace the skins in the vessel in which they were soaked, cover them with boiling water, stir and bruise well so as to extract the juice completely, then strain through the sieve or bag. Mix this preparation with the juice, add the sugar, and sufficient boiling water to increase the liquid to 5 gallons.

Replace in the bowl or tub, stir in the cream of tartar, cover with a heavy woollen cloth, and allow the vessel to stand in a moderately warm place for 2 days. Now strain the liquid into a small cask, cover the bunghole with a folded cloth until fermentation ceases—which may be known by the cessation of the hissing noise—then bung closely, but provide the bung of the cask with a vent-peg. Make this wine in the beginning of June, before the berries ripen; let it remain undisturbed until December, then drain it off carefully into a clean cask.

In March or April, or when the gooseberry bushes begin to blossom, the wine must be racked off into bottles and tightly corked.

Store it in a cool, dry place.

GOOSEBERRY WINE (Another Method)

Ingredients.—Firm green gooseberries. To each lb. of fruit allow 2 pints of cold water. To each gallon of juice obtained from the fruit allow 3 lb. of loaf sugar, ½ a pint of good gin, ¾ of an oz. of isinglass.

Method.—Top and tail the gooseberries, bruise them thoroughly, pour over them the cold water, and let them stand for about 4 days, stirring frequently. Strain through a jelly-bag or fine hair sieve, dissolve the sugar in the liquid, add the gin and isinglass dissolved in a little warm water, and pour the whole into a cask. Bung loosely until fermentation has ceased, then tighten the bung, and let the cask remain undisturbed for at least 6 months. At the end of this time the wine may be bottled, but it will not be ready for use for at least 12 months.

GRAPE WINE

Ingredients.—Sound, not over-ripe grapes; to each lb. allow
1 quart of cold water. Add to each gallon of liquid obtained
from the grapes 3 lb. of loaf sugar, ¼ of a pint of brandy, and
about a ¼ of an oz. of isinglass.
Method.—Strip the grapes from the stalks, put them into
a wooden tub or earthenware bowl, and bruise them well
with a wooden mallet or pestle. Pour over them the water,
let them stand for 3 days, stirring frequently, then strain
through a jelly-bag or fine hair sieve. Dissolve the sugar in
the liquid, then pour the whole into a cask. Bung lightly
for a few days until fermentation subsides, then add the
isinglass dissolved in a little warm water, and the brandy,
and tighten the bung. Let the cask remain undisturbed for
6 months, then rack the wine off into bottles, cork and seal
them securely, and keep for at least a year before using.
Note.—If the grapes are very sweet one might dispense
with the sugar.

GRAPE WINE (*Unfermented*)

Ingredients.—15 lb. of stalked and crushed grapes, 4½ lb. of
loaf sugar, 1 pint of water.
Method.—Put the crushed grapes and water into a preserving-pan and cook over gentle heat until the pips have sepa-
rated from the pulp. Strain through a fine sieve or jelly-
bag, stir in the sugar and cook over gentle heat until it
reaches boiling point, stirring continuously and removing
the scum as its rises. Pour into bottles while still hot, cork
and seal.

LEMON WINE

Ingredients.—10 lemons, 4 lb. of loaf sugar, 4 quarts of
boiling water, dried yeast. (See Instructions, Page 15.)
Method.—Remove the rinds of 5 lemons in thin fine strips.

and place them in a wooden tub or earthenware bowl. Boil the sugar and water together for ½ an hour, then pour the syrup over the lemon-peel. When cool add the strained juice of the 10 lemons, add the yeast, and let the vessel stand for 48 hours. At the end of this time strain into a cask, which the wine must quite fill, bung loosely until fermentation ceases, then tighten the bung, and allow the cask to remain undisturbed for about 6 months before racking the wine off into bottles.

MEAD

Ingredients.—5 lb. of honey, 3 gallons of water, the whites of 2 eggs, 1 blade of mace, ½ an inch of cinnamon, 3 cloves, ¾ an inch of whole ginger, dried yeast. (See Page 15.)
Method.—Beat the whites of eggs slightly, put them into a large pan with the water, honey, mace, cinnamon, cloves and ginger, whisk or stir frequently till boiling-point is reached, then simmer gently for 1 hour. Let the preparation cool, strain it into a cask, add the yeast, cover the bunghole with a folded cloth until fermentation ceases, then bung tightly, and let the cask stand in a cool, dry place for 9 months. At the end of this time rack the mead carefully into bottles, and cork them tightly. The mead may be used at once, but it will keep good for years, if stored in a cool, dry place.

MEAD WINE

Ingredients—5 gallons of water, 5 lb. of honey, 2 oz. of dried hops, yeast on toast.
Method.—Dissolve the honey in the water, add the hops, and simmer very gently for 1 hour, turn into an earthenware bowl, let it become milk-warm, then add the yeast. Allow it to remain covered for 3 days, then strain the liquid

into a cask, bung loosely until fermentation subsides, and afterwards tighten the bung.

The wine should remain in the cask for 12 months, and then be racked off carefully into bottles.

MULBERRY WINE

Ingredients.—3 gallons of sound ripe mulberries, 3 gallons of water. To every gallon of liquid allow 4 lb. of loaf sugar. 1 quart of brandy and 1 oz. of isinglass.

Method.—Crush the mulberries in a large basin or tub and pour over them the water. Let stand for at least 24 hours, stirring from time to time. Strain through a fine sieve, measure the liquid and stir in sugar in the proportion stated above. When this has dissolved pour into the basin or tub again, cover with a clean cloth and let it stand to ferment for 5 days. Now strain into a clean cask, keeping back a pint or two of the liquid to fill up the cask as fermentation subsides. As soon as the hissing has entirely ceased add the isinglass dissolved in a little of the wine and the brandy. Secure the bung and bottle at the end of a year.

NECTARINE WINE

See recipe for Peach Wine, and use nectarines in place of peaches.

ORANGE WINE

Ingredients.—The juice of 50 Seville oranges, 15 lb. of loaf sugar, 4 gallons of water, the whites and shells of 3 eggs, 1 pint of brandy, 3 tablespoonfuls of yeast.

Method.—Dissolve the sugar in the water, add the whites and crushed shells of the eggs, bring to the boil, and simmer gently for 20 minutes. Let it stand until nearly cold, then strain through a jelly-bag, add the strained orange-juice and yeast, and leave the vessel covered for 24 hours. Pour into a cask, bung loosely until fermentation subsides, then tighten the bung, and allow the cask to remain undisturbed for 3 months.

At the end of this time rack it off into another cask, add the brandy, let it remain closely bunged for 12 months, then bottle and use as required.

PARSNIP WINE

Ingredients.—4 lb. of parsnips, 3 lb. of demerara sugar ¼ of an oz. of mild hops, dried yeast on 1 slice of toasted bread, 4 quarts of boiling water.

Method.—Boil the parsnips gently in the water for 15 minutes, add the hops, and cook for 10 minutes longer. Strain, add the sugar, let the liquid become lukewarm and put in the toast spread with the yeast. Let it ferment for 36 hours, then turn it into a cask, which it should fill.

As soon as fermentation ceases, strain into bottles, cork lightly at first (see Instructions, Page 17), and store in a cool dry place for at least 1 month before using.

PEACH WINE

Ingredients.—12 lb. of sound, ripe peaches, 6½ lb. of loaf sugar, 2½ gallons of water, 3 small eggs, a little yeast, 2 oranges, 1 lemon, 1 pint of brandy, ½ oz. of gelatine, and ¼ oz. of candy sugar.

Method.—Cut the peaches into slices and place them in a large bowl with 2½ lb. of crushed sugar sprinkled over them. Let them remain undisturbed for at least 24 hours. Boil the water and stir in 4 lb. of sugar and the stiffly whisked whites of the eggs and cook for 20 minutes, removing the scum as it rises. Now add the peaches and sugar and continue to boil until the fruit is all reduced to a pulp, removing the scum as it rises. Remove the peach stones and crush them. Put them into a large bowl or tub and pour over them the hot fruit pulp that is in the cooking pan. Let the bowl or tub stand until the contents are lukewarm, then add the yeast. Cover over with a clean cloth and let it remain undisturbed for 3 or 4 days. Strain through a sieve and pour into a clean cask, keeping back about a quart of the liquid to fill up the cask as fermentation subsides. Add the strained juice and the thinly peeled rinds of the oranges and lemon. As soon as the hissing has ceased pour in the brandy and secure the bung.

Let the cask stand for 2 months, then rack the wine off and filter the lees. Pour the wine back into the cask together with the dissolved gelatine and sugar candy. Secure the bung and leave the cask undisturbed for at least 6 months. The wine may then be bottled and the corks sealed. It should be kept at least for another 6 months before it is taken into use.

PLUM WINE

Ingredients.—As for Peach Wine, but substitute plums for peaches.

The weight of plums to the gallon is an individual matter, for, by increasing the plums, this wine can be made to resemble a port. Generally speaking, 12 lb. to the gallon makes a good, burgundy strength of wine. Indeed, with certain kinds of plums, the matured wine is not dissimilar to a burgundy.

Method.—Put the plums in the fermenting vessel or vessels and pour over them the proportionate amount of boiling water. Then squeeze and stir the pulp daily for about six days, as suggested in the 'working example' in the Instructions, Page 19.

In fact, follow these instructions, and you can hardly go wrong. Victoria plums are good for the purpose, but any fleshy variety will do.

QUINCE WINE

Ingredients.—1 gallon of fresh quince juice, 5 lb. of loaf sugar, and 2 quarts of brandy.

Method.—Pour the quince juice into a large bowl or tub and stir in 4 lb. of the sugar, previously crushed. Cover with a clean cloth and leave undisturbed until it has finished fermenting. Then drain off the liquid and stir in the remainder of the sugar (crushed) and when the latter has dissolved pour in the brandy. Bottle carefully and seal the corks securely.

RAISIN AND ELDERBERRY WINE

Ingredients.—18 lb. of raisins, 1 gallon of sound, ripe elderberries, 2½ lb. of loaf sugar, 4½ gallons of boiling water, 1 orange, 3 lemons, 1 pint of brandy, ½ oz. of isinglass, 3 oz. of sugar candy.

Method.—Bruise the elderberries and put them into a large bowl or tub with the crushed sugar sprinkled over. Stir well and let stand for 24 hours. Next stone and chop the raisins and turn them into another tub, pouring the boiling water over them. Stir well, cover with a clean cloth and let stand for 24 hours.

Now boil the elderberries and sugar for ½ an hour, skimming from time to time as necessary and at the end of that time strain the liquid into the other tub with the raisins. Stir well for about 30 minutes and then cover with a clean cloth and allow to stand undisturbed for 3 days.

Strain the liquid off into a clean cask, keeping back about 2 or 3 pints in order to fill up the cask as fermentation subsides.

Add the thinly peeled rind of the orange and lemons and when the hissing has quite ceased pour in the brandy. Secure the bung and let the cask remain undisturbed for 2 months.

Now rack off the wine and filter the lees. Pour the wine back into the cask and add the isinglass dissolved in a little of the wine together with the sugar candy. Secure the bung.

The wine will be ready to bottle in about 10 months and the bottles should be kept another six months before being taken into use.

RAISIN WINE

Ingredients.—To each lb. of raisins allow I gallon of cold water, 2 lb. of preserving sugar, dried yeast, see Page 15.

Method.—Strip the raisins from the stalks, put them into a large boiler or clean copper with the water, simmer gently for about 1 hour, then rub them through a sieve. Dissolve the sugar in the liquid, and add the raisin-pulp and the yeast, let the vessel stand covered for 3 days, then strain the liquid into a cask.

Bung loosely until fermentation ceases, then tighten the bung, and allow the cask to stand for at least 12 months before racking the wine off into bottles.

RAISIN WINE (*Another Method*)

Ingredients.—16 lb of raisins, 2 gallons of water.

Method.—Strip the raisins from the stalks, put them into an earthenware or wooden vessel, pour over them the water, and let them remain covered for 4 weeks, stirring daily. At the end of this time strain the liquid into a cask which it will quite fill, bung loosely until fermentation subsides, then tighten the bung, and allow the cask to remain undisturbed for 12 months.

Now rack it off carefully into another cask, straining the liquid near the bottom of the cask repeatedly until quite clear, let it stand for at least 2 years, and then bottle for use.

RASPBERRY WINE

Ingredients.—10 quarts of ripe raspberries, 10 quarts of boiling water, 6 lb of good preserving sugar, 1 pint of brandy, ¼ of an oz of isinglass.

Method —Prepare the fruit in the usual way, put it into an earthenware or wooden vessel, pour over it the boiling water, and let it remain covered until the following day. Pass both liquid and fruit through a fine hair sieve, let it stand for 24 hours, then strain it carefully into another vessel, without disturbing the sediment. Add the sugar, and as soon as it is dissolved, turn the whole into a clean, dry cask. Cover the bung-hole with a folded cloth until fermentation subsides, then bung it closely Let it stand for 1 month, rack it off into a clean cask, add the brandy and isinglass dissolved in a little warm water, bung tightly, and allow it to remain undisturbed for 12 months.

At the end of this time rack it off into bottles, cork securely, store for 12 months longer, and the wine will be ready for use.

RASPBERRY WINE (*Another Method*)

Ingredients.—6 quarts of ripe raspberries, 6 quarts of water, loaf sugar.

Method.—Put the raspberries into an earthenware or wooden vessel, bruise them well with a heavy wooden spoon, and pour over them the cold water. Let them stand until the following day, stirring them frequently, then strain the liquid through a jelly-bag or fine hair sieve, and drain the fruit thoroughly, but avoid squeezing it. Measure the liquid; to each quart add 1 lb. of sugar; stir occasionally until dissolved, then turn the whole into a cask.

Bung loosely for several days, until fermentation ceases, then tighten the bung, let it remain thus for 3 months, and bottle for use.

RED CHAMPAGNE

Ingredients.—1½ lb. of beetroots, 5 gallons of sound, ripe green gooseberries, 5 gallons of water, 15 lb. of loaf sugar, 1 oz. of bruised ginger, 2 lemons, 1 oz. of isinglass, 1 pint of brandy.

Method.—Boil the beetroots gently for about 20 minutes, being careful not to break the skins. When cold slice them and put them into a tub with the picked and mashed gooseberries. Pour over them the water and stir well. Cover the tub with a clean cloth and let stand for 4 days, stirring from time to time. Strain through a sieve or jelly bag and pour into a clean cask, adding the crushed sugar, the ginger, the thinly peeled rind of the lemons and the isinglass, dissolved in a little of the liquid. Let it stand until the hissing has entirely ceased and then pour in the brandy. Secure the bung.

The wine will be ready to bottle in 12 months' time. Seal and fasten the corks of the bottles with wire. The wine should be kept at least 6 months in the bottles before being taken into use.

RHUBARB WINE

Ingredients.—25 lb. of rhubarb, 5 gallons of cold water: to each gallon of liquid thus obtained add 3 lb. of either loaf or good preserving sugar, and the juice and very thinly-pared rind of 1 lemon. To the whole add 1 oz. of isinglass.

Method.—Wipe the rhubarb with a damp cloth, and cut it into short lengths, leaving on the peel. Put it into an earthenware or wooden vessel, crush it thoroughly with a wooden mallet or other heavy instrument, and pour over it the water. Let it remain covered for 10 days, stirring it daily; then strain the liquor into another vessel, add the sugar, lemon-juice and rind, and stir occasionally until the sugar is dissolved. Now put it into a cask, and add the isinglass previously dissolved in a little warm water; cover the bung-hole with a folded cloth for 10 days, then bung securely, and allow it to remain undisturbed for 12 months. At the end of this time rack off into bottles, and use.

ROWAN WINE

Ingredients.—4 gallons of sound, ripe rowan berries, boiling water, loaf sugar. To every gallon of wine allow 1 oz. of isinglass and 1 pint of brandy.

Method.—Gather the rowan berries on a fine, dry day. Bruise them well and place them in a tub. Just cover with boiling water. Cover the tub with a clean cloth and let it stand undisturbed for 3 days. Carefully remove the scum and strain the liquid through a sieve into a large basin, measuring it carefully. To every gallon of liquid allow 1 lb. of crushed loaf sugar. Stir until it is thoroughly dissolved, then pour the wine into a clean cask, keeping back a quart or so to fill up the cask as fermentation subsides. As soon as the hissing has entirely ceased, pour in the dissolved isinglass and brandy. Secure the bung. The wine will be ready to bottle at the end of 6 months.

SAGE WINE

Ingredients.—20 lb. of raisins, 1½ pecks of fresh, green sage leaves, 4½ lb. of honey, 5 gallons of water, 5 eggs, 2 oranges, 3 lemons, 1 oz. of isinglass, and 1 pint of brandy.

Method.—Stir the honey and whites of the eggs into the water and boil for an hour, removing the scum as it rises. Put the stoned and chopped raisins with the shredded sage leaves into a tub and pour the boiling liquid over them. Cover with a clean cloth and let stand for 2 days, stirring from time to time. Strain off the liquid through a fine sieve, crushing the fruit and leaves thoroughly in order to extract all the juice. Leave this over-night and after 12 to 18 hours pour the clear liquid into a clean cask, being careful not to disturb the sediment and keep back about a quart of the liquid to fill up the cask as fermentation subsides. Filter the lees and add the liquid to the cask together with the strained juice and the thinly peeled rind of the oranges and lemons. Do not bung the cask but fill up as fermentation subsides and as soon as the hissing has ceased pour in the brandy and isinglass, dissolved in a little of the wine. Secure the bung and bottle at the end of 12 months.

SLOE WINE

Ingredients.—4 gallons of sound, ripe sloes, 4 gallons of boiling water. To every gallon of liquid allow 4 lb. of loaf sugar. To every 3 gallons of wine allow ½ oz. of isinglass and 1 quart of brandy.

Method.—Crush the fruit and put it into a tub with the boiling water. Let it stand for 5 days, stirring from time to time. Strain off the liquid and measure it. Add sugar in the proportion stated above and stir until it is dissolved. Pour the liquid into a clean cask, reserving a quart or so to fill up with as fermentation dies down. Keep the cask filled up and as soon as the hissing ceases, pour in the brandy and dissolved isinglass. Secure the bung and bottle at the end of 2 years or less if the wine seems clear.

STRAWBERRY SACK

Ingredients.—Sound, ripe strawberries, sherry. To every pound of fruit allow 4 oz. of sugar candy.

Method.—Pack the strawberries into wide-mouthed bottles, adding crushed sugar candy in the proportion stated above and fill up the bottles with sherry. Cork securely and let stand for at least 3 months, shaking the bottles from time to time.

At the end of 3 months filter the liquid and bottle.

STRAWBERRY WINE

Ingredients.—6 gallons of sound, ripe strawberries, 6 gallons of water, 4 gallons of cider (optional), 2 oz. of cream of tartar, 2 lemons, 16 lb. of loaf sugar, 1 quart of brandy and 1 oz. of isinglass.

Method.—Crush the fruit and put it with the water into a large bowl or a tub. Let it stand undisturbed for a day and a night, then strain the liquid off into a clean cask. Add the cider, tartar, the thinly peeled rind of the lemons and the sugar. As soon as the hissing has entirely ceased pour in the brandy and the dissolved isinglass. Secure the bung and bottle at the end of a twelve month.

TURNIP WINE

Ingredients.—Turnips and crushed loaf sugar. To every gallon of juice allow 3 lb. of loaf sugar and ½ pint of brandy.

Method.—Wash, peel and slice the turnips thinly, sprinkle over them a little crushed sugar and let them remain until next day. Pound and squeeze out as much juice as possible, measure and pour it into a clean cask. Add sugar and brandy in the proportion stated above. Keep the cask filled up while the wine is working and as soon as fermentation has ceased secure the bung. The wine will be ready for bottling at the end of 3 months. It should be kept for another 12 months before use.

Lightning Source UK Ltd.
Milton Keynes UK
UKOW04f1309150913

217217UK00001B/18/P